4521586   LEE
388.842
-0 MAY 1976

D1580173

HERTFORDS.

This book is due for return on or before the date shown. You may extend its loan by bringing the book to the library or, once only, by post or telephone, quoting the date of return, the letter and number on the date card, if applicable, and the information at the top of this label.

**The loan of books in demand cannot be extended.**

**RENEWAL INFORM- ATION**

L.32A

- FEB. 1973    Please return to
POTTERS BAR CRANBORNE
53788

1 6 APR 2003

- OCT. 1972
- NOV. 1973

4 MAY 2002    /.

1 - 9 APR 2007

2/6

# IOO YEARS
# OF THE DISTRICT

*Price Three Shillings and Sixpence*

*The illustration on the cover is
the District Railway armorial device*

*All the photographs in this book are from London Transport records,
except Plates 1, 2, 3, 4 and 23 which are from the author's own collection*

# 100 Years

# of the

# District

by

Charles E. Lee, M. Inst. T.

LONDON  TRANSPORT

55 Broadway, Westminster, SW1

SBN 85329 0113

HERTFORD
COUNTY LIB

4521586
388.42

POTTERS BAR
CRANBORNE

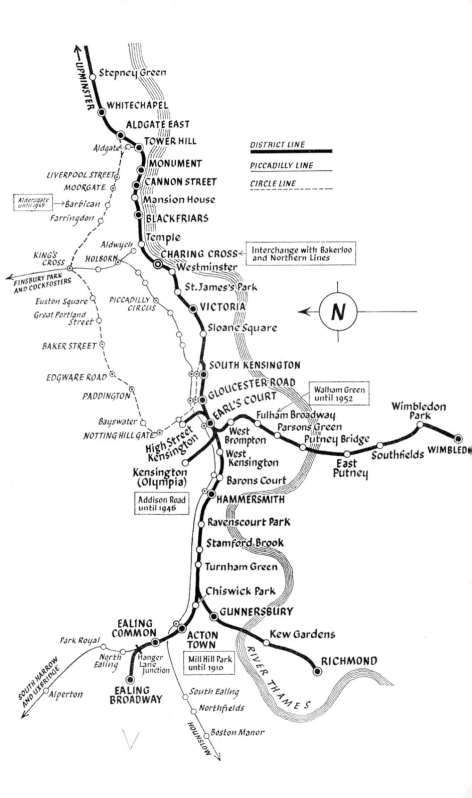

# 100 Years
# of the
# District

When the first section of the District Line was opened, one
hundred years ago, few could have envisaged that this was the
beginning of a great urban railway, destined to become a
pioneer of transport co-ordination and the nucleus of London
Transport. It had its origin in the spate of railway promotions
in the early 1860s shortly after the opening on 10 January 1863
of the original section of the Metropolitan Railway, the first
urban underground railway in the world. This extended from
Bishop's Road, Paddington, to Farringdon Street and at first
was closely associated with the Great Western Railway. It was
laid with mixed-gauge tracks to accommodate both the broad-
gauge (7 ft.) trains of the G.W.R. and also standard-gauge
(4 ft. 8½ in.) trains of other railways. From the outset, the
G.W.R. maintained the service, but friction arose between
the companies, and the Metropolitan began working its own
line on 11 August 1863.

Powers had already been secured for the extension of the
original lines at both ends, and in November 1863 a separate
scheme, called 'Metropolitan District Railways', was promoted
to complete an inner circle of railways north of the Thames,
and an outer circle round the Metropolis by means of a series of
connecting lines to existing railways. The engineer was John
Fowler (afterwards Sir John). As Parliament in the Session of
1864 was presented with no fewer than 259 different projects
for making about 300 miles of railway in and about London, it
set up a joint committee which advised that many of the

schemes should not be entertained. One to emerge successfully from this scrutiny was that for completing an inner circle. In the outcome, the Metropolitan Railway was authorized to build the sections from Paddington to South Kensington, in the west, and to Aldgate and Tower Hill, in the east. Both Acts received the Royal Assent on 29 July 1864.

The separate scheme was divested of its outer circle proposals, and was consolidated with a rival called the Metropolitan Grand Union Railway. In this form, it was incorporated as the Metropolitan District Railway Company by another Act of 29 July 1864, with powers to complete the Inner Circle between South Kensington and Tower Hill, with spurs from South Kensington (duplicating the authorized Metropolitan Line as far as Gloucester Road) to a junction with the West London Extension Railway at West Brompton; and from Kensington High Street to a junction with the West London Railway near Addison Road. Although a separate company, the Metropolitan District Railway board included four Metropolitan Railway directors, and had the same engineers, namely, John Fowler as Engineer-in-Chief, and T. Marr Johnson. Both during the construction stages, and even after the first section was opened, the 'District Railway', as it was always termed, was generally regarded as virtually part of the Metropolitan, and their amalgamation when the Inner Circle was complete was widely expected.

No time was lost in proceeding with the work of construction. A contract was made in February 1865 with a consortium of firms comprising Peto & Betts, Kelk, and Waring Brothers, for the line from Kensington to Cannon Street, and the first sod was cut at Kensington on 29 June 1865. As the whole line was intended to be in a shallow subway, it was built on the cut-and-cover method whereby an excavation was lined with side walls and roofed over with brick arching or girders to enable the surface to be restored. There are no true tunnels on any part of the District Line portion of the Inner Circle. With a route near the north bank of the Thames, the line necessarily crossed a number of old streams, and one of these, the Westbourne (encased as the Ranelagh sewer), passes over Sloane Square station at an angle in an 86 ft. length of cast-iron pipe, 9 ft. in diameter. Counter's

Brook crosses the railway west of Earl's Court station; the Tyburn to the east of Victoria station; and the Fleet to the west of Blackfriars station.

Where the line runs under Parliament Square, special provision was made to reduce delays to surface traffic to the minimum, and also to give special protection to Westminster Abbey. The length of 330 yd. (of which 308 yd. was girder-covered way, and 22 yd. arched tunnel) was completed in six weeks during severe winter weather, in accordance with an agreement made with the parish authorities whereby heavy penalties would have been incurred for every 24 hours of delay. For some 99 yd. adjacent to Westminster Abbey, a packing of peat, 7 ft. thick, was introduced behind the south wall of the tunnel to reduce the vibration of passing traffic. After having served for 100 years, some of the girder-covered sections of tunnel roof on the District Line are being strengthened to meet modern road traffic requirements and the new standards for bridges and structures set by the Ministry of Transport. Work was begun in June last (1968) near the corner of Broadway and Tothill Street, and the whole programme will be undertaken, stage by stage, over a period of years.

Comparatively few physical difficulties were encountered, but there were numerous and lengthy delays in acquiring property. Also, during the progress of the works, the country was plunged into the great financial panic of 1866, precipitated by the failure of Overend, Gurney & Co. on 10 May. The bank rate rose to 10 per cent. and remained at that figure for three months, the longest period ever. At least 13 other banking houses, and numerous contractors, failed in the chain reaction, with Peto & Betts among the casualties. Sir Samuel Morton Peto and Edward Ladd Betts retired from the contracting consortium and were replaced by Charles Thomas Lucas and Thomas Lucas. The eastern end of the Inner Circle beyond Mansion House was abandoned temporarily, although some work had already been done at Cannon Street.

The western extension of the Metropolitan Railway was brought into use from Edgware Road to Gloucester Road on 1 October 1868, but no part of this was District Railway property. Efforts to get part of the District Line ready for the Christmas traffic included employing nearly 3,000 men day and night for the last month, and on 24 December 1868 it was opened from South Kensington to Westminster Bridge (as the station was called until 1907) at the same time as the link of the Metropolitan Railway between Gloucester Road and South Kensington. Under an agreement of 1866, the Metropolitan worked and maintained the District lines as they were opened for traffic. The service was regulated by a joint committee, and the Metropolitan paid the District 55 per cent. of the gross receipts, whether from local traffic or on the proportion of through traffic. From the opening, the District was worked by Metropolitan Railway stock, consisting of four-wheel coaches hauled by Class A 4-4-0 condensing tank locomotives designed by John Fowler and built by Beyer, Peacock & Co. Ltd.

At Westminster Bridge station a pedestrian subway to the Houses of Parliament was built during the latter part of 1868, and brought into use with the opening of Parliament on 8 February 1870. Public access to part of this subway was given in September 1934, when a new entrance was made on the south side of Bridge Street. The body of William Ewart Gladstone, the great statesman, was conveyed through this subway on 25 May 1898, when it was brought by rail from Hawarden to lie in state for two days in Westminster Hall.

A further section of the District Railway was opened on 12 April 1869. This was the one mile from Gloucester Road to West Brompton, which was worked by a shuttle service. Through trains did not run to West Brompton until 1 August 1870, two months after the Blackfriars extension was opened, and these Blackfriars to West Brompton trains (of course, worked by the Metropolitan) seem to have been the first to make regular use of the southern pair of tracks between South Kensington and Gloucester Road. At West Brompton the connection with the West London Extension Railway was never made (although the powers were kept alive until 1893) and the trains terminated at a separate station. It had been intended that trains of the London, Brighton & South Coast Railway and the London & South Western Railway should run over the District by this route, but negotiations fell through.

Eastward of Westminster Bridge, the railway was destined to run under the proposed Thames Embankment, the great work of Sir Joseph Bazalgette which had been authorized by the Thames Embankment (North) Act of 1862. As early as March 1865, the Metropolitan Board of Works had asked the District Railway directors when they would be in a position to begin work on their line between Westminster and Blackfriars, but Fowler decided that it would be unwise to begin until the Embankment was built, the water excluded, and the filling nearly completed. The Embankment was opened as a footway on 30 July 1868, and thus was available for pedestrians when the District Railway was opened to its Westminster Bridge station. In July 1869, the capital for the railway extension from Westminster Bridge to Cannon Street was raised by the issue of 5 per cent. preference stock, and work was begun on 9 August. By reason of financial and other difficulties, the section was completed only as far as Blackfriars, to which it was opened on 30 May 1870, a remarkable achievement in so short a time. The Embankment itself was opened for vehicular traffic on 13 July 1870 by the Prince of Wales (afterwards King Edward VII) and was named the Victoria Embankment. The average height of the rails under the Embankment is 13 ft. below water of the River Thames.

Meanwhile, the independent directors of the District Railway had become dissatisfied with the working of their line by the Metropolitan, and formal notice of the intention to terminate the working agreement was served on 3 January 1870, to become effective on 3 July 1871. The Metropolitan directors on the District Board resigned, and the District appointed its own Managing Director in the person of James Staats Forbes, General Manager (and later Chairman) of the London, Chatham & Dover Railway, who continued his association with that company. It was a step that was to lead to the development of the District Railway, not only as an independent enterprise but also as the active (and at times bitter) competitor of its erstwhile parent.

Its first great moment as an independent enterprise was the formal opening on Saturday, 1 July 1871, of the extension from Blackfriars to Mansion House, which, although a distance of only 31 chains, was described by *The Engineer* as 'the most important event of the year, in connection with additional railway accommodation in London'. It had been built in three months from the time the company had secured possession of the property. The Rt. Hon. W. E. Gladstone, the Prime Minister, who was present as a shareholder at the opening banquet, said that 'the underground railway illustrated the present wants and destinies of London, the vast need that is felt for an increase in the means of locomotion, and the novel and unheard-of resources that it is developing for the purpose of meeting the necessity'. Public traffic began on the Monday, 3 July, and the District Railway began operating its own line, although the Metropolitan continued to run over it between South Kensington and Mansion House. Before the opening, Mansion House station had been referred to as the Cannon Street terminus. It was at the intersection of Cannon Street and the newly-built thoroughfare called Queen Victoria Street (from Blackfriars Bridge to the Mansion House) which was completed on 4 November 1871. An unsuccessful attempt was made by the District Railway to extend its line to a site nearer to the Bank, and all thoughts of completing the Inner Circle seem to have been in abeyance.

When the District arranged to work its own system, it ordered from Beyer, Peacock & Co. 24 similar locomotives to those used by the Metropolitan. They were built in 1871 at a contract price of £2,280 each. The District remained faithful to the type throughout its steam days, and augmented the stock from the same builders by batches of half a dozen in 1876, 1880, 1883, 1884, and 1886, bringing the total to 54. The livery was a dull green. In later years, the District weather boards (there were no cabs) differed from the plain straight ones of the Metropolitan in being bent back over the footplate. Repair shops and sheds were built at West Brompton, which became known as the Lillie Bridge depot. The walls were entirely of concrete, and these were probably the largest buildings that had so far been erected in that material. Fowler was a pioneer in its use.

Three classes of coaches were used, all four-wheel stock, 26 ft. 6 in. long. The initial stock was 38 first-class, 38 second-class, 76 third-class, totalling 152. First-class coaches had four compartments seating five a side; they were roomy and well upholstered. The second- and third-class had five compartments, seating five a side. Third-class upholstery was confined to a strip of carpet on the seat, and a padded back strip at shoulder

12

1. Building the line by the cut-and-cover method near Gloucester Road in 1866. The double-line twin tunnels are being roofed with five-ring brick arching laid on temporary iron centrings

2. Excavation scene, with steam crane, looking east along Victoria Street from a point near the junction with Vauxhall Bridge Road

3. Street elevation of Gloucester Road station shortly before completion in 1868

4. Gloucester Road station nearing completion; it was opened on 3 October 1868. The elliptical roof of iron arched-rib construction between vertical retaining walls was typical of the original sub-surface stations

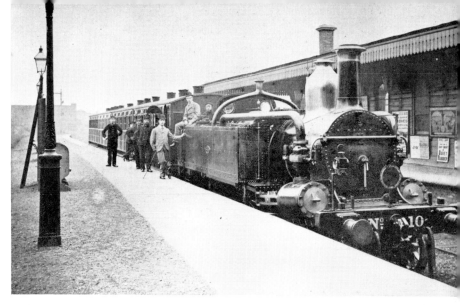

5. Steam train in the spring of 1876 at West Brompton station, then the terminus of the line. The locomotive is one of the batch built in 1871, and is in its original form.

6. Earl's Court old station in May 1876. The top-hatted figure is Thomas Samuel Speck, the first Locomotive Superintendent and Resident Engineer. This station was opened on 31 October 1871, on the east side of Earl's Court Road. Its modest timber building was destroyed by fire on 30 December 1875. On 1 February 1878 it was replaced by a new station on the west side of Earl's Court Road. Coincidently, the first burrowing junction on the system was brought into use at Cromwell Road

7. ABOVE Platform view at Mansion House in 1896. The first 'penny-in-the-slot' machine on a British railway station was installed at Mansion House in July 1886. It was a wooden machine, and at first was called a 'chocolate box'

8. Mansion House station in 1903

9. Mansion House station in 1956

10. Embankment frontage to Charing Cross station in 1903. The arched roof of the South Eastern Railway station (now Southern Region), which may be seen on the left, collapsed on 5 December 1905

11. The same scene in March 1960

12. Sloane Square station about 1890

13. Sloane Square station in 1954, after post-war rebuilding

14. Interior of the old Sloane Square station in June 1926, showing prominently in the foreground the cast-iron pipe carrying the water of the old Westbourne (encased as the Ranelagh sewer) across the station

height; second-class equipment was slightly more generous. Trains were first lighted by coal gas carried in bags on the coach roofs, but in 1878 Pintsch compressed-oil gas at about 90 lb. per sq. in. was substituted.

Both the District and the Metropolitan were in a poor financial position in the early 1870s, and each was seeking additional sources of traffic. Sir Edward Watkin of the South Eastern Railway on 7 August 1872 became Chairman of the Metropolitan also. He was known already to be a keen opponent of Forbes, and any willing co-operation between the two companies during their respective reigns proved impracticable. The District sought to extend its activities to the south-west of London, which was expanding as a prosperous residential district. The London & South Western Railway had already occupied much of the territory with a series of lines opened in the 1860s, but its terminus at Waterloo on the south side of the Thames was not convenient for the City. On 1 January 1869, the L.S.W.R. had opened a railway from Kensington (Addison Road) to Richmond, which later was to play a vital part in the history of the District Line, but its access to the City was at Ludgate Hill, reached from Kensington by a lengthy route through Brixton which involved two crossings of the river.

The District was a financial failure from the viewpoint of the shareholders. It was paying no dividend on its ordinary stock and therefore could not raise new capital for extensions, except by forming separate companies. Some of these secured Parliamentary approval for lines which were never built, but gave bargaining power to the District in its relations with the L.S.W.R., and it is sufficient for our present purpose to record what was achieved. Westward of Earl's Court, the link to Addison Road had been built in 1869, but was not regularly used until 1 February 1872, when the London & North Western Railway began working an Outer Circle service from Broad Street to Mansion House, *via* Willesden and Addison Road. The Great Western Railway inaugurated a Middle Circle service on 1 August 1872, running from Mansion House to Addison Road, Paddington, and Moorgate. From a junction with the Addison Road link line, the first of the new District Railway extensions was opened to Hammersmith on 9 September 1874 and was claimed to offer communication from the City 'superior in expedition and convenience to the Metropolitan Company's route from Moorgate Street'.

Then the L.S.W.R. agreed to give to the District running powers from Hammersmith to Richmond, so long as this route should be the only access to Kew, Richmond, and beyond, to be used by the District. This Hammersmith junction line from Hammersmith to Ravenscourt Park (until March 1888 called Shaftesbury Road) was opened on 1 June 1877 and District trains were extended to Richmond. With the aid of these running powers, the District promoted a line from Turnham Green to Ealing Broadway, which was opened on 1 July 1879. This was a distance of 2 miles 75 chains and was the longest section so far opened by the company at one time. A plan to extend to Uxbridge was opposed successfully by the G.W.R., but the latter afterwards allowed District trains to run from Mansion House, through Ealing, to Windsor. The service was not well patronized, possibly because District Railway rolling stock did not ride well on the non-stop run between Ealing and Slough on the main-line railway; the venture lasted only from 1 March 1883 to 30 September 1885.

Still with an eye to suburban extension, the District arranged to prolong its short West Brompton branch (which had never served its originally-intended purpose) to Putney Bridge. This was opened on 1 March 1880, and attracted unexpectedly heavy traffic. It also provided the jumping-off point for the eventual service to Wimbledon. Before this, however, the route mileage worked by the District had been increased by six miles with the opening of the Hounslow branch. This was promoted by local landowners as a separate company but was worked by the District, which did not acquire the ownership until 1903. The line was opened from Mill Hill Park (which was re-named Acton Town on 1 March 1910) to Hounslow Town (old station) on 1 May 1883, and through trains were worked to and from Mansion House only until 4 December of that year. Thereafter, throughout the days of steam operation, Hounslow trains ran only to Earl's Court. A branch was built from Osterley to Hounslow Barracks (re-named Hounslow West on 1 December 1925) and opened on 21 July 1884. The original terminal station of Hounslow Town was closed on 31 March 1886 in favour of a new station on the Hounslow Barracks line called Heston Hounslow (which became Hounslow Central in the re-namings of 1925).

In the changed circumstances that the District Railway (as also the Metropolitan) was devoting its attention to serving suburban residential traffic, there was no enthusiasm for completing the Inner Circle, and the District powers east of Mansion House were allowed to lapse in 1870. Independent City interests formed their own company to build the missing link, but failed to raise the capital. Eventually, the need to meet a clearly-expressed public requirement, and the desire to avoid the incursion of another company, caused the District and the Metropolitan to enter into an uneasy partnership. By an Act of 11 August 1879 the two companies jointly secured new powers for the missing link between Mansion House and Aldgate, and also for an extension to join the East London Railway near Whitechapel. The works proved very costly, and involved the building of a new street, Byward Street. Contributions from public authorities assisted, but the reluctant railways regarded the whole undertaking as a heavy burden.

Under its earlier unexpired powers, the Metropolitan hastily built the section from Aldgate to Tower Hill, which it opened to a temporary station on 25 September 1882. The remainder of the scheme was brought into use on 6 October 1884, the Mansion House to Tower Hill portion making the Inner Circle a reality at last, and the line to Whitechapel giving both the District and the Metropolitan access to the East London Railway. The District maintained a Hammersmith-New Cross service from 6 October 1884 to 31 July 1905. With the completion of the Inner Circle, the District and the Metropolitan both worked their trains all round; heretofore the Circle trains (a name familiar since 1871 for what was really a horseshoe service) had been provided and staffed by the Metropolitan. The temporary station at Tower Hill (which bore the name Tower of London station) was made redundant by the new joint station called Mark Lane, opened with the completion of the Circle. Nevertheless, the Metropolitan kept it open for a week until 13 October 1884, although its existence was ignored by District trains. The temporary wooden surface building survived until August 1940, and more recently the site has taken on a new lease of life.

The last extension of District passenger services in the nineteenth century was made as a result of another arrangement with the L.S.W.R. Joint schemes were discussed which would have given the District running powers to Surbiton, using a new line from Fulham, and also have admitted L.S.W.R. trains to South Kensington. Instead, the L.S.W.R. built the railway from Putney Bridge to Wimbledon and granted running powers to the District. This line was opened on 3 June 1889 and District trains thereafter ran to Wimbledon. Although built and owned by the L.S.W.R., the section from Putney Bridge to East Putney, including the trellis-girder bridge over the Thames, was never used by L.S.W.R. trains.

Despite its chronic impecuniosity, and the conditions of 'cold war' which applied to its relationships with the Metropolitan, the District Railway during the nineteenth century exercised considerable enterprise and ingenuity in extending its system and attracting traffic. In 1900 it carried 43,842,000 passengers, and the average service interval on the Mansion House to South Kensington section was $3\frac{1}{4}$ minutes. It sponsored various bus services, which were maintained by contractors for such purposes as feeders to its system and also to serve exhibition traffic. For many years, a major source of District traffic was derived from exhibitions. The earlier ones were at South Kensington, on the then-open grounds to the south of the Albert Hall. The District built a pedestrian subway from South Kensington station, running under Exhibition Road, to serve such traffic, and a toll of a penny was charged. It was opened on 4 May 1885 (the opening day of the Inventions Exhibition), but was closed on 10 November 1886, with the finish of this series of exhibitions. Thereafter, it was used only on special occasions until it was thrown open free to the public on 21 December 1908. Another kind of exhibition, and one which became a noteworthy feature of London life, as well as an important source of revenue to the District, was opened at Earl's Court on 9 May 1887 on land rented from the District; a covered way from Earl's Court station to Warwick Road was brought into use on the same day. A once-famous landmark at Earl's Court was the Big Wheel, which was brought into use on 6 July 1895 and lasted until 12 October 1906.

Relationships with the Metropolitan became less tense after the resignation of Sir Edward Watkin in 1894 from the chairmanships of that company and of the S.E.R., as a result of his incapacitation by a stroke. At the same period, increasing bus competition, the promotion of tube railways, and the impending construction of electric tramways, impelled the District to consider many plans of development. These included further extensions to Harrow and Uxbridge in the west, and a link with the London, Tilbury & Southend Railway in the east. To reach Harrow, a separate company was formed in 1894, which made a working agreement with the District. The line was built in 1898-9, but was not then brought into use; it was vested in the District in 1900. Onwards to Uxbridge the railway was in the hands of another company, promoted by local landowners interested in the development of the neighbourhood. It made a working agreement with the District, but, while the difficulties of finance were being overcome, the scheme passed into the sphere of the Metropolitan (with which it was to be linked at Harrow on the Hill), leaving the District with running powers.

In the east of London, a company called the Whitechapel & Bow Railway had secured powers in 1897 for a 2-mile underground line. The company was controlled jointly by the District and the L.T.S.R., but the line was to be worked by the District. This was the first of the District extensions planned as a tunnel or covered way. All the westward extensions were almost entirely open, sometimes in shallow cutting, but largely on viaduct. When the City Lines & Extensions were opened in 1884, the District Railway had also built a 12-chain terminus at Whitechapel for its exclusive use, and not part of the joint ownership. This spur was used as the beginning of the new Whitechapel & Bow line, upon which construction was begun in May 1899.

Another scheme of 1897 was for a deep-level 'electric express' line in tube beneath the existing Earl's Court to Mansion House section, to duplicate facilities over the busiest part of the system. There was to be only one intermediate station, at Charing Cross. The District Railway obtained its Act for this on 6 August 1897, and two years later the authorized Brompton & Piccadilly Circus Railway secured sanction to form a junction with it at South Kensington. The whole scheme remained in abeyance. One reason for deferring the deep-level project was that general electrification of the system, with automatic signalling, was regarded as a better way of increasing the working capacity of the undertaking. The use of electric battery locomotives had been considered early in 1888 and rejected.

Track electrification would necessarily involve agreement with the Metropolitan as to the system of electric traction to be used on the Inner Circle. The two companies experimented by equipping with third rail on the direct-current system the Earl's Court to High Street line (fed by a small temporary power station at Earl's Court), at a cost of £20,000. Tests began in February 1900, and public traffic was carried from 21 May to 6 November, at first at the 'novelty' fare of 1s. single, and subsequently at normal fares. Eventually, the District and the Metropolitan set up a joint committee which recommended the adoption of the three-phase a.c. 3,000-volt system (with overhead conductor wires) developed by Ganz of Budapest. In February 1901, the Metropolitan accepted the recommendation, but the whole matter was thrown into the melting pot by a change in ownership of the District.

The background to this change, which has had a profound effect on the shape of transport developments in London during the present century, is to be found in the international financial situation at the turn of the century. A burst of activity in the early 1890s had resulted in Parliament sanctioning numerous deep-level electric tube railways, for which there was an undoubted traffic need, but which proved unattractive to the investing public. The period was one of great industrial company promotions, and a generation of colourful 'promoters' presented their prospects of speculative financial hopes on a far higher scale than could reasonably be expected from an urban railway, particularly on the showing of the existing ones. Throughout its independent career, the District paid dividends on its ordinary stock on only five occasions, and the highest distribution was $1\frac{1}{8}$ per cent. in

1880. Even the $4\frac{1}{2}$ per cent. first preference stock never received its full dividend after 1884.

On the other hand, the U.S.A. was approaching saturation in domestic expansion and was embarking on world investment. The representative of some wealthy and powerful U.S.A. syndicates, in the person of Charles Tyson Yerkes, who had had experience over a quarter of a century in the traction business, decided to examine the possibilities of rejuvenating and expanding transport in London. Initially, he bought the powers for the Hampstead Tube on 1 October 1900 for £100,000. His introduction to the District seems to have been on the invitation of Robert William Perks (afterwards Sir Robert), a London solicitor who had acted for the Hampstead Railway and also held a substantial amount of District Railway stock. With the aid of Perks, Yerkes was able to secure effective control of the District in March 1901, and immediately announced his intention to modernize the line and proceed with the conversion to electric traction. Forbes retired from the chairmanship that he had held for 29 years, and was succeeded for a short time by Murray Griffith, a stockbroker who had taken an important part in securing control for the American interests. Griffith handed over the chair to Perks on 5 September 1901, but remained a director for more than 30 years.

Yerkes and his group proceeded to form the Metropolitan District Electric Traction Co. Ltd., which was incorporated on 15 July 1901, to effect the electrification of the District and to build a power station (on land to be bought by the District under its statutory powers and conveyed to the Traction Company) which would supply current to the District and to the proposed Brompton & Piccadilly Circus tube, another acquisition of the group. On 9 April 1902, the Underground Electric Railways Company of London Ltd., a very much larger concern, was incorporated to take over the M.D.E.T. The principal parties to the new company were Yerkes himself, Speyer Brothers of London, Speyer & Co. of New York, and the Old Colony Trust Company of Boston. A little later, the Amsterdam house of Teixeira de Mattos Bros. participated. In a statement issued to the shareholders in April 1903, Yerkes said: 'In acquiring all these lines, it has been our desire to form a perfect system of intramural transportation, and to have them all feed into the District Railway, and be fed by the same line'.

By this time the Underground Company had also secured control of the Baker Street & Waterloo Railway (partly built by other interests, but upon which work had been suspended); the Great Northern & Strand Railway (a scheme which was merged with the Brompton & Piccadilly Circus to form the nucleus of the present Piccadilly Line); and the London United Tramways Ltd. (which had a system of electric tramways based on Shepherd's Bush and Hammersmith that was being extended rapidly in the Thames Valley area, and also to Uxbridge). The Underground had already begun work in March 1902 on the great power station at Lots Road, Chelsea, and undertook to construct and equip the tube railways, as well as to electrify the District. In regard to the last-named, Yerkes and his friends were entirely out of sympathy with the relatively-untried Ganz system of electrification, and favoured low-voltage direct current as already adopted on the Central London Railway, and used extensively in the U.S.A. As the Metropolitan adhered to its decision to adopt the joint committee recommendation, the matter was referred to arbitration and the award was in favour of the District. Yerkes offered to take over the Metropolitan on lease at a guaranteed fixed and perpetual dividend of $3\frac{1}{2}$ per cent., but this was refused.

Hitherto, the third-class fares on the District had been influenced by a rigid adherence to the Parliamentary penny-a-mile, but one of the earliest steps taken after the change in control was a drastic lowering of fares on 1 May 1901 in an effort to recover the traffic that had been lost to the buses and to the Central London Railway. The latter had been opened on 30 July 1900 from the Bank to Shepherd's Bush, and immediately earned itself the name of the 'Twopenny Tube' by charging a uniform fare of 2d. for any distance and having only one class of passenger. The District made a second fare reduction on 1 June 1902 and secured a considerable increase in the number of passengers, but not sufficient to avoid a drop in total receipts. The numbers of passengers rose from 42,268,000 in 1901 to 47,015,000 in 1902, to 50,040,000 in

15. ABOVE Aldgate E
old station in 1903;
station was opened
6 October 1884

16. Aldgate East in 19

17. BELOW Aldgate E
in July 1957. The stat
was rebuilt on a new s
eastward of the old
and opened on 31 Octo
1938

18. View in 1906 of Chiswick Park station, opened on 1 July 1879 as Acton
Green. It was still a typical suburban station. It bore the name Chiswick Park &
Acton Green from March 1887 to March 1910, when it became Chiswick Park

19. Chiswick Park station in March 1933, after entire reconstruction in
reinforced concrete during 1931-32 in connection with the quadrupling west of
Hammersmith. The architects were Messrs. Adams, Holden & Pearson

20. Boston Manor station in December 1930. It was opened as Boston Road on 1 May 1883, and renamed Boston Manor on 11 December 1911. The reconstruction of the station was completed on 25 March 1934

21. Platform view of South Ealing station in 1934. The original station was opened on 1 May 1883. It was rebuilt in 1932 in connection with the quadrupling of the line between Acton Town and Northfields, preparatory to the extension of Piccadilly Line trains to Hounslow

22. New canopy and waiting room at Hounslow East station in 1965

23. Prominent direction signs at the corner of Dacre Street and New Tothill Street (now Dean Farrar Street) in July 1898

24. Austere interior of a third-class compartment of steam stock

25. District Railway station at Blackfriars about 1876. The ornate superstructure was destroyed during the second World War. Blackfriars was the eastern terminus of the railway from its opening on 30 May 1870 until the extension to Mansion House was brought into use on 3 July 1871

26. Wooden control trailer of 1905 electric stock, built to American design. As built, these had a luggage compartment, which was later removed

27. A five-car train of 1920 all-steel stock with rounded roof, outside Ealing Common depot

28. The first unpainted aluminium train on London Transport railways, composed of Class R stock, at Ealing Broadway

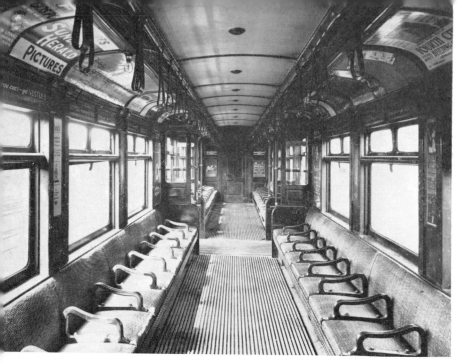

29. Interior of motorcar of the original Class B stock introduced in 1905 for the general electrification of the system

30. A modern interior. The Class R stock

1903, and to 51,168,000 in 1904, the last year of all-steam operation.

Another effort to increase revenue was the introduction of a parcels delivery service in November 1902, using tricycle carriers for delivery. This was hailed in the contemporary press as 'a fresh example of the enterprise of the District Railway under its present chairmanship'. The venture lasted only until 18 March 1905, when it was withdrawn because the management felt that, with electric traction, its activities should be confined to passenger traffic. A further change of this period was the introduction of a full service of trains on Sundays from 26 July 1903. District services, like those of other local lines, had previously been suspended on Sunday mornings for 'church hours' between 11 a.m. and 1 p.m.

The Whitechapel & Bow Railway, built at a cost of £1,200,000, was opened on 2 June 1902. Initially, District trains ran over the new line and thence over the Tilbury line as far as East Ham, with a few through to Upminster. The Tilbury section to East Ham was quadrupled under powers of 31 July 1902, which also authorized electrification. The one remaining extension, which had been built but not opened, was that from Ealing to South Harrow. This line was the first to be electrified and was used for training motormen for the main electrification. Current was obtained from a temporary generating station at Alperton, until the inauguration of the Lots Road Power House on 1 February 1905. The short section from Ealing (Hanger Lane junction) to Park Royal was brought into public service on 23 June 1903 in connection with the Royal Agricultural Society's Show at Park Royal, and thus became the first portion of the District to be placed under permanent electric operation. Public service was extended to South Harrow on 28 June 1903.

Electrification of the District was carried out under the direction of James Russell Chapman, an American electrical engineer who was one of the chief officers of the Yerkes syndicate and was responsible for the whole of the equipment of the railways in the group. He was Engineer-in-Chief and General Manager of the Underground Company. It was on the 600-volt direct-current system, for use mainly by multiple-unit trains. The complete conversion was brought into use during 1905, towards the end of which year the last steam trains were withdrawn. Third and fourth rails were used, with the positive 16 in. outside the track (and 3 in. higher), and the negative in the centre, $1\frac{1}{2}$ in. higher than the running rails. These current rails were of flat-bottom type, weighing 100 lb. a yard, laid on porcelain insulators. The original running rails of the District had been 83 lb. flat-bottom steel rails spiked direct to transverse sleepers. From 1873 they had been replaced gradually by 83 lb. bull-head rail in cast-iron chairs. Much of the track was relaid for electrification, using 86 lb. rails in 48 lb. chairs.

The first section of the District to be *converted* to electric traction was the Hounslow branch. An electric service from South Acton to Hounslow Barracks was begun on 13 June 1905. This involved opening to passengers on that date the South Acton branch, built in 1899. (This branch is now abandoned; the last trains ran on 28 February 1959.) The original spur to Hounslow Town (old) station, derelict since 1886, had been re-opened on 1 March 1903. For electrification, a 7-chain curve towards Hounslow Barracks was laid, and this enabled trains to run into and out of the Town station, where they reversed. The arrangement was not long-lived, for Hounslow Town terminal station was finally closed on 1 May 1909 and replaced by a new through station on the main line which was re-named Hounslow East on 1 December 1925.

Electric traction on the District main line from Ealing to Whitechapel was introduced on 1 July 1905. High Street, Kensington to Putney Bridge followed on 23 July, and the electrification of the L.S.W.R. line enabled electric services to be extended to Wimbledon on 27 August. Equipment of the L.S.W.R. line between Turnham Green and Richmond allowed a through Richmond to Whitechapel service to be begun on 1 August. The electric extension eastwards of Whitechapel, over the lines of the Whitechapel & Bow and the L.T.S.R., was brought into use to East Ham on 20 August; the Upminster steam trains were withdrawn on 30 September. With the Inner Circle service, electric trains were introduced gradually between 13 September and 24 September. All steam trains were withdrawn from the District on 5 November, excepting those of the L.N.W.R. Outer Circle service, and these were hauled electrically east of Earl's Court from 4 December.

New multiple-unit open stock was adopted, and compartment stock disappeared from the District, excepting on foreign trains. Provision was made for first- and third-class passengers, but the old second class was abolished from 1 July 1905. (Although Gibb forecast its early demise in August 1907, first-class accommodation lasted throughout the separate life of the District, but was withdrawn by London Transport as from 1 February 1940, in war conditions, and never restored.) The first electric stock was of gate-platform type. It was used first on the South Harrow line, and subsequently also for local services on the Hounslow branch. The last cars of this class were withdrawn in 1925. The original electric rolling stock ordered for the main electrification consisted of 420 vehicles (making 60 seven-car trains) of American design, based on that used by the Brooklyn Elevated Railway. The rattan-covered seats were mostly longitudinal.

For electric traction it was decided to adopt a system of automatic signalling controlled by track circuits, based on that of the Boston Elevated Railway which in 1901 had brought into use the first installation of its kind. It was introduced on the Hounslow line on 11 June 1905 and throughout the main District system on 14 January 1906, as a result of satisfaction with the experimental installation on the South Harrow line from its opening in 1903. The essential features of this Westinghouse electro-pneumatic system are the use of signals and train stops actuated by the passage of trains. Signalmen are eliminated except at junctions and regulating points. The system involves the use of a normal 'clear' aspect instead of a normal 'danger'. When there is no train in a section, the aspect is 'clear', but the presence of a train sets the signal to 'danger' in rear of that train. A pivoted arm alongside the rails, working in conjunction with the signal, rises above rail level when the signal goes to 'danger', and engages a trip cock on the train, which applies the brakes if a motorman endeavours to run past.

Electro-pneumatically-operated semaphore signals were used on all the open sections of line, and the last of these (at Hanger Lane junction, Ealing) survived until November 1953. In tunnel, the signals took the form of a single lamp with moveable spectacle mechanism containing the coloured glasses.Multiple-aspect colour-light signals began to be adopted in 1923 in tunnel sections, and are now universal. From the outset, the signalling system included the then novel feature of illuminated track diagrams in the signal boxes; the first in the world was introduced by the District Railway on 5 June 1905.

Yerkes himself had assumed the chair of the District Railway in February 1905 and had the satisfaction of seeing opened the Lots Road power station, then stated to be 'the largest in the Old World', and steam eliminated from the District. He last attended a board meeting of the Underground Company on 7 November 1905, and then went on a visit to New York where he died on 29 December. Edgar Speyer (created a baronet in July 1906) became financial head of the group, as Chairman of the Underground Company, with Sir George Stegmann Gibb (heretofore General Manager of the North Eastern Railway) as Deputy Chairman & Managing Director. Sir George also became Chairman of the District Railway, and held that office until 1910.

With various tube railway schemes now under the same financial control as the District, the earlier railway could no longer be regarded in isolation. By an agreement of 1902, the District undertook to provide the Piccadilly Line with a link between Earl's Court and West Kensington and to transfer to the Piccadilly its existing powers for a deep-level line between South Kensington and Earl's Court. By an Act of 1904 the District was also authorised to acquire land to widen its line between West Kensington and Hammersmith to afford separate access tracks to Hammersmith for Piccadilly trains. The District reserved running powers against the eventual building of its own deep-level line to Mansion House, but abandoned that scheme in 1908.

The immediate task of the Gibb regime was to complete and open the tube railways of the group. On 10 March 1906 the first section of the Baker Street & Waterloo Railway was opened, extending from Baker Street to Kennington Road (now Lambeth North). It quickly caught the public fancy, and the late Captain G. H. F. Nichols ('Quex' the diarist) devised the shortened title 'Bakerloo' in the columns of the *Evening News*. This was adopted by the company, for popular use, in July

1906, to the keen dislike of some of the more sedate British railway officers. More than sixty years later, this happy invention is the official title of the Bakerloo Line. The new tube fed the District Railway at Charing Cross, where it shared the station facilities. Next came the Piccadilly Line, opened from Finsbury Park to Hammersmith on 15 December 1906, and intimately associated with the District at its western end, as already indicated.

Finally, the Hampstead Tube between the Strand and Golders Green, with a branch from Camden Town to Highgate (now Archway), was brought into use on 22 June 1907, and was publicized as 'The Last Link'. At the inaugural luncheon, the keynote of the official speeches was that, 'with the opening of this line, the great work undertaken by the Underground Electric Railways Company of London has been completed'. For the first few years, the Hampstead Tube did not meet the District anywhere. It was the last of the Yerkes railways to be brought into use, although it was the first scheme in London in which he became interested. Gibb was instrumental in the establishment in July 1907 of the London Passenger Traffic Conference, which inaugurated a period of closer working between all the various London underground railways, irrespective of financial control.

At this period, a new and dynamic personality came on the scene, with the appointment of Albert Henry Stanley (1874-1948), later Lord Ashfield, as General Manager of the Underground Group. He took up his duties as General Manager of the District Railway on 26 September 1907, and became Managing Director in May 1910. Stanley was born in Derby, but spent his early business career in the United States, where he rose from humble beginnings with the Detroit Street Railway Company to become General Manager of the Public Service Corporation of New Jersey. An early important step which he is said to have inspired was the use of a general distinctive symbol for all the underground railways of London, whether within his own group or not. This was adopted at a meeting of the London Passenger Traffic Conference on 29 February 1908, and took the form of an illuminated sign bearing the word UNDERGROUND with large initial and final letters, which thereafter was exhibited at all stations (even surface ones) and survives, with slight modification in design, as the symbol of the London Transport railways.

On 16 December 1907 the whole train service of the District (except the Inner Circle service, which was worked wholly by Metropolitan stock) was revised and much improved. A feature of the new arrangements was the introduction of non-stop trains during peak hours. The island platform layout at Earl's Court enabled some fast trains to overtake and pass stopping trains there. After the L.T.S.R. line from East Ham had been quadrupled, and Barking station rebuilt, the District electric service was extended to Barking on 1 April 1908. In May 1908 the District introduced a nine-car train between Whitechapel and Barking, which was claimed to be the longest multiple-unit train in the world in regular operation. Then in May 1909 a ten-car train was run from East Ham to Whitechapel, and there divided. Platform lengths on the tunnel section restricted normal trains to seven or eight cars, but some ten-car trains were introduced in 1910, and the two rear cars stopped in the tunnel.

Increased traffic with electrification taxed to its utmost capacity the two-track L.S.W.R. line between Studland Road junction (near Hammersmith) and Turnham Green, which then was also used by L.S.W.R. and G.W.R. passenger trains, as well as by Midland Railway coal trains. A proposal by the District in 1902 to build its own tracks had been opposed by the L.S.W.R., but eventually a widening was agreed between the two companies, and authorized by Parliament in 1910. The widened lines were opened on 3 December 1911, with a burrowing junction at Turnham Green. Thereafter, District trains had the exclusive use of the southernmost pair of tracks, but ownership of all four was vested in the L.S.W.R. A new station called Stamford Brook was built on the southern pair of tracks only and was opened on 1 February 1912. The additional lines enabled substantially increased services to be introduced on 11 December 1911, with many more non-stop trains.

Although flat junctions were laid in all cases when the system was built, a burrowing junction was brought into use on 1 February 1878 at Cromwell Road (east of Earl's Court). This was the only example on the District in the days of steam traction. Flying junctions at Acton Town were opened on

10 February 1910 when that station was re-built with an altered layout; Ealing and Hounslow trains were thus segregated. Another burrowing junction, to the west of Earl's Court, was brought into use on 4 January 1914. This enabled the Wimbledon services to be operated without causing delay to those from Hammersmith and beyond.

On the underground section of the District, stations were in open cuttings so far as possible, with vertical retaining walls and elliptical roofs of iron arched-rib construction with a span of 50 ft. 6 in. Station platforms were 300 ft. long. At Temple station a flat roof had to be built because an agreement with the Duke of Norfolk (whose property the line crossed here) provided that this station should not have a raised roof. Surface buildings were usually single-storey structures of simple design, but many of the frontages were nearly covered by notice boards and posters. After electrification, the stations underwent considerable improvement. Repainting, cleaning, and electric lighting was undertaken throughout the system, and, where possible, the old arched roofs were removed. As early as 1908 automatic ticket-issuing machines were installed.

As from 1 July 1910 the three separate tube companies of the group were merged as the London Electric Railway. By reason of their separate promotion, there was no traffic connection originally between the Hampstead Tube and either the Bakerloo or District Lines, although they were within a short distance of one another at Charing Cross. To improve the interchange facilities, the L.E.R. promoted a short extension of the Hampstead Tube under Villiers Street to the Embankment, making a terminal loop. A single-platform station was arranged underneath the District Line, and Charing Cross underground station was rebuilt as part of this work to serve as an adequate exchange station for the three railways (Bakerloo, District, Hampstead). With the rebuilding, a circulating area was made under the District tracks, and connected with the two tube stations by pairs of escalators. The loop line was opened on 6 April 1914, and the station was given the new title of Charing Cross (Embankment), although this addition to the name lasted only until 9 May 1915.

On the outbreak of war, the District came under Government control on 5 August 1914, and this remained until 15

August 1921. Sir Albert Stanley (he was knighted in 1914) left the Underground group in December 1916 to become President of the Board of Trade. He returned as Chairman in August 1919 and was raised to the peerage in 1920 as Lord Ashfield of Southwell. Post-war rehabilitation affected the tube railways and road transport services much more than it did the District, but towards the end of 1920 the first of new all-steel cars came into service. These had elliptical roofs, instead of the clerestory roofs used on all previous electric stock. By eliminating running boards, these cars were 11 in. wider than previous ones. The running board has never returned, but the next new batch of cars (1923-24) reverted to the clerestory roof.

Through the aid of the Trade Facilities Act of 1922, which enabled the necessary finance to be raised with a Government guarantee, the L.E.R. planned a 2-mile extension of the Hampstead Tube from its terminus at Charing Cross to a junction and interchange station at Kennington with the City & South London Railway, that had come into the group in 1913. This link, as also a 5-mile extension from Clapham Common to Morden, was brought into service on 13 September 1926. The Hampstead Tube and the C. & S.L.R. were thereby integrated into one system, which has been known since August 1937 as the Northern Line. This resulted in additional traffic of about 26,000 passengers a day at Charing Cross, and necessitated the further reconstruction of the underground station. Work was begun in 1926, and the various new features were introduced piecemeal so as to reduce to the minimum any inconvenience to existing traffic. By March 1929 virtually a new station had emerged. An enlarged circulating area had been built beneath the District Line tracks; additional escalators had been installed; and a new booking hall built.

The Developments (Loans, Guarantees and Grants) Act of 1929 was passed with the principal object of relieving the pressure of the unemployment problem, and this provided the opportunity to initiate various much-needed schemes of transport development. One which affected the District Line was the widening to four tracks of the $4\frac{1}{2}$-mile section from Hammersmith to Northfields to provide for the through running of Piccadilly Line trains over the District to

Hounslow and South Harrow. This was the expansion of a scheme which had been contemplated before the first World War, when, by an Act of 1913, powers had been secured to build an extension from the Piccadilly Line station at Hammersmith to link up with the L.S.W.R. Kensington-Richmond branch. Here the war had altered the whole situation, as the L.S.W.R. Kensington-Richmond service had run for the last time on 3 June 1916, and its tracks between Hammersmith and Turnham Green were little used. The Southern Railway (successor to the L.S.W.R.) in 1932 granted the District Railway a long lease of these lines, and Southern staff was replaced by District staff. The four tracks were rearranged for parallel working; two lines, with intermediate stations, were designed to serve the District traffic, and the other two a new non-stop Piccadilly Line service. Chiswick Park station was entirely reconstructed with platforms on the District Line only, and a new eastbound platform for District trains was built at Stamford Brook. Work was begun in the autumn of 1930 and proceeded rapidly. Piccadilly Line trains were extended to Acton Town and South Harrow on 4 July 1932, and thence to Uxbridge (after the formation of London Transport) on 23 October 1933. (Thereafter, District services did not work beyond Ealing.) The Hounslow branch of the District was quadrupled between Acton Town and Northfields on 18 December 1932, and Piccadilly Line trains ran through to Northfields from 9 January 1933; they were extended to Hounslow West on 13 March 1933.

Meanwhile, important developments were taking place in East London. The L.T.S.R. had been taken over by the Midland Railway in 1912, and Parliament had imposed the obligation on the new owners to prepare a scheme for the electrification of the direct line from Fenchurch Street to Southend. The first World War intervened, and no such plan was ever submitted to Parliament. In order to relieve the Southend main lines of local traffic, however, the London, Midland & Scottish Railway (into which the Midland had been merged) widened its line between Barking and Upminster to four tracks. The new tracks were equipped for electric traction to enable District trains, previously terminating at

Barking, to run through to Upminster. Colour-light signalling and automatic train stops were also installed. New stations were built at Upney and Heathway; Becontree replaced Gale Street Halt; and Dagenham, Hornchurch, and Upminster were completely reconstructed. The new electric train services to Upminster were brought into operation on 12 September 1932. (Since nationalization, the L.T.S. line, which is now part of the Eastern Region of British Rail, has been converted to electric traction on the a.c. overhead system, and the full electric train service from Fenchurch Street to Southend and Shoeburyness was introduced on 18 June 1962.)

With the establishment of the London Passenger Transport Board by Act of 13 April 1933, the District Railway and its associated tube railways, the Metropolitan Railway, the principal bus undertakings, and both company and municipal tramways came under unified ownership from 1 July 1933. A pool was established with the suburban lines of the main-line railways, and it became economically possible to plan transport on a broader basis. With the aid of Government guarantee, a a great scheme of improvements and extensions (originally estimated to cost £40 million) was launched. As with the 1929 scheme, the effect on the District Line was much less than elsewhere, but station reconstruction in the central area included District stations at Earl's Court, Sloane Square, Monument, and Aldgate East. The works at Aldgate East were far more extensive than ordinary station reconstruction, as they involved building a new station on a site to the east of the old one, and the construction of a new south curve so as to widen the triangle and enable eight-car trains to be accommodated between the junctions, instead of six-car. The new Aldgate East station was opened on 31 October 1938, and the new south curve was brought into service four weeks later.

At Sloane Square, the rebuilt station was opened on 27 March 1940, and included escalators from the platforms to the street. These were the first escalators to be built for District Line traffic; the first railway escalator in London had been brought into use at Earl's Court on 4 October 1911, between the District and Piccadilly Lines, and the banks of escalators at Charing Cross have already been mentioned, but all these were to serve the tube railways. The new Sloane Square station was destroyed by a direct bomb hit on 12 November 1940. The station remained open with improvised facilities. After the war, it was again rebuilt, and the new works were completed on 3 May 1951.

At nationalization on 1 January 1948, the London Passenger Transport Board was replaced by the London Transport Executive of the British Transport Commission. Lord Ashfield had been appointed the first Chairman of the L.P.T.B. and remained at the helm almost to the end. He resigned the chairmanship as from 31 October 1947, having been appointed a Member of the B.T.C., and died on 4 November 1948. On 1 January 1963 London Transport reverted to its original status as an independent statutory undertaking called the London Transport Board.

The recent opening of part of the new Victoria Line has rightly directed public attention to the extended use of automatic facilities, but it is worthy of record that important experimental work in this field was undertaken on the District Line. The first experiments in automatic train operation were made between Stamford Brook and Ravenscourt Park, beginning on 8 April 1962. An automatic ticket barrier was first used at Stamford Brook station on 5 January 1964, and the large-scale use of automatic ticket gates for ingoing passengers, with additional automatic ticket and change-giving machines, began at Hammersmith (District and Piccadilly Lines) on 19 March 1967.

For more than 80 years the 'City terminus' of the District Line was at Mansion House. With the completion of the Inner Circle, two tracks became through lines, but it remained the only station with terminal platforms and lines for westbound trains. In recent years, office rebuilding in the City has resulted in traffic increases which made it desirable to have the terminal facilities further east. The site selected for the new station is one of considerable historical interest, as it is immediately adjacent to remains of the Roman wall of Londinium, and also is the place where the short-lived Tower of London station was located. It was decided to build a new station here in replacement of the old Tower Hill station (until 1 September 1946 called Mark Lane), and the construction involved some delicate operations, including the underpinning of the 1914-18 Merchant Navy War Memorial. The new Tower Hill station was opened on 5 February 1967, and the terminal and reversing facilities there came into use on 21 January 1968, although a few trains still turn at Mansion House. The 'City terminus' has thus been moved some 57 chains further east, and the total cost of the work was about £1,750,000.

On reaching its centenary, the District Line is a unit of the London Transport Board working some 30 route miles of railway, and providing a vital link in the co-ordinated chain of urban transport facilities serving the metropolis.

269/675RP/2500     Printed in Great Britain by The Parcener Press Ltd., London, S.E.27